Mary A.clapp

BOB MENENDEZ

ADVOCATE FOR IMMIGRATION RIGHTS

Mary A.clapp

Mary A. Clapp

All right reserved. No part of this book may be reproduced, distributed,or other electronic mechanical methods, without the prior written permission of the publisher, except in the case of brief quotation embodied in the critical reviews and certain other non-commercial uses permitted by copyright law

Copyright @.Mary A.Clapp,2024

Mary A.clapp

Mary A.clapp

TABLE OF CONTENTS

INTRODUCTION

CHAPTER 1: EARLY LIFE AND CAREER

PRIORITIES IN POLITICS

PARTICIPATION IN NATIONAL POLITICS

CHAPTER 2: IMMIGRATION POLICY BEGINNINGS

ORIGINAL IMMIGRATION STANCE

EARLY POSITIONS AND EFFORT IN THE LAW

CHAPTER 3: MAJOR LEGISLATIVE EFFORTS

INTERNATIONAL RELATIONS

LAWSUIT POSITIONS AND EFFORTS

CHAPTER 4: ADVOCACY AND PUBLIC STANCE

Mary A.clapp

PROMOTING IMMIGRATION REFORM ADVOCATES

WORKING WITH GROUPS THAT ADVOCATE FOR IMMIGRATION

PART IN SENATE HEARINGS AND COMMITTEES

CHAPTER 5: CHALLENGES AND CONTROVERSIES

OPPOSITION TO POLITICS

DISPUTES AND CRITICISMS ABOUT IMMIGRATION POLICIES

CHAPTER 6: KEY ACHIEVEMENTS AND IMPACTS

CONSUMER PROTECTION AND ECONOMIC POLICY

SUCCESSFUL CHANGES IN POLICIES AND LAWS

WHAT HAPPENS TO IMMIGRANT COMMUNITIES

CHAPTER 7: CASE STUDIES

COMPREHENSIVE IMMIGRATION REFORM CASE STUDY

BOB MENENDEZ'S ROLE

Mary A.clapp

CHAPTER 8: FUTURE LOOK

PERMANENT RESEARCH AND INITIATIVES

FUTURE LEGISLATION PROSPECTS

LEGACY AND IMPACT ON IMMIGRATION REFORM
OVER TIME

CONCLUSION

Mary A.clapp

WHO IS BOB MENENDEZ?

American politician Bob Menendez represents New Jersey as a U.S. senator. senator. He was raised in Union City, New Jersey, after being born in New York City on January 1, 1954. Since January 2006, he has been a member of the Democratic Party and the Senate. Prior to serving in the Senate, Menendez was a member of the New Jersey General Assembly and the mayor of Union City, among other local and state political roles, during his term in the U.S. House of Representatives from 1993 to 2006.

Menendez is well-known for his contributions to immigration, finance, healthcare, and international policy. In addition to leading the Senate Foreign AffairsAffairs Committee, he has been actively involved in significant legislative initiatives pertaining to foreign affairs, healthcare policy, and immigration reform.

Mary A.clapp

Menendez is still a prominent player in American politics in spite of going through legal difficulties, including accusations of corruption for which he was found not guilty.American politician Bob Menendez represents New Jersey as a U.S. senator. senator.

He was raised in Union City, New Jersey, after being born in New York City on January 1, 1954. Since January 2006, he has been a member of the Democratic Party and the Senate. Prior to serving in the Senate, Menendez was a member of the New Jersey General Assembly and the mayor of Union City, among other local and state political roles, during his term in the U.S. House of Representatives from 1993 to 2006.

 Menendez is well-known for his contributions to immigration, finance, healthcare, and international policy. In addition to leading the Senate Foreign AffairsAffairs Committee, he has been actively involved in significant legislative initiatives pertaining to foreign affairs, healthcare policy, and immigration reform. Menendez is still a prominent player in American politics in spite of going through legal difficulties, including

Mary A.clapp

accusations of corruption for which he was found not
guilty.

Mary A.clapp

INTRODUCTION

One of the main priorities of Senator Bob Menendez's legislative agenda is immigrant rights, for which he has long been known as a staunch supporter. His professional background and personal history, which combine his wealth of public service experience with his Cuban immigrant parents' origins, form the foundation of his unwavering dedication to this cause.

 Menendez has continuously put the interests and rights of immigrants first throughout his political career because he recognises their vital role in the fabric of American society. He has devoted his life to addressing

Mary A.clapp

the problems encountered by immigrant communities and advocating for all-encompassing changes that will establish a more fair and reasonable immigration system. His work has been distinguished by his emphasis on protecting undocumented minors, reuniting families, and providing millions of undocumented immigrants with a road to citizenship.

Menendez's work on immigration is driven by his belief in the American Dream and the country's reputation as a land of opportunity, and it goes beyond simple policy advocacy. He has gained notoriety in the current national immigration debate as a result of his legislative proposals and lobbying, which emphasize the significance of social justice, economic contributions, and human rights in determining U.S. immigration policy.

Mary A.clapp

CHAPTER 1: EARLY LIFE AND CAREER

CHILDHOOD AND FAMILY BACKGROUN

On January 1, 1954, Bob Menendez was born in New York City to Evangelina and Mario Menendez, immigrants from Cuba. After his family relocated to Union City, New Jersey, he grew up in a working-class area. Menendez's upbringing in an immigrant household gave him a profound appreciation for the struggles and

Mary A.clapp

goals faced by immigrant groups. Menendez's parents, a carpenter and seamstress, put in a lot of effort to support their family. Their commitment to creating a better life for themselves in America had a significant impact on Menendez's morals and work ethic. Menendez's strong sense of justice and dedication to public duty were shaped by seeing his parents' hardships and tenacity.

Even with those financial difficulties, Menendez was a stellar student. During his time at Union Hill High School, he showed promise as a leader and a strong interest in community involvement. He continued his education after high school, graduating from Rutgers School of Law with a law degree and Saint Peter's College in Jersey City with a bachelor's degree.

His personal encounters with the difficulties experienced by immigrant families and his upbringing in an immigrant family would subsequently influence his political career and his passionate support of immigration rights. His eventual position as a U.S. senatorial senatorial advocate for the immigrant community was made possible by these early influences.

Mary A.clapp

PRIORITIES IN POLITICS

Bob Menendez's early political career was strongly influenced by the challenges and goals of his neighborhood. His dedication to serving the public and his desire to meet the needs of his people were the defining characteristics of his early political activity. Menendez began his political career in the 1970s by participating in Union City, New Jersey, local politics. He became one of the youngest elected politicians in the history of the state when he was elected to the Union City Board of Education at the age of just 19. His early encounter gave him a platform to speak out in favor of better educational policies and to meet the needs of kids from a variety of backgrounds.

Because of Menendez's unwavering commitment to his community, he was elected mayor of Union City in 1986. He prioritized advancing economic development, enhancing public services, and reviving the city during his time in office. He developed a reputation as a

Mary A.clapp

conscientious and capable leader due to his hands-on style and attentiveness to regional issues. Menendez increased his influence in politics in 1987 when he was elected to the New Jersey General Assembly, a position he held until 1991. He was able to work on more general policy concerns, such as healthcare, education, and economic development, throughout his term in the state legislature while still keeping his people's needs front and center. Menendez was elected to the New Jersey State Senate in 1991 as a result of his expanding influence and dedication to public service.

His tenure in the state legislature served to further establish his standing as an ardent supporter of his community, especially with regard to issues impacting working families and immigrants. Menendez's path of early political engagement laid laid the groundwork for his subsequent responsibilities in national politics and his unwavering dedication to social justice and immigration rights. His early triumphs and experiences in municipal and state administration gave him the knowledge and understanding needed to successfully negotiate the difficulties of the federal legislative system

Mary A.clapp

and effectively represent his constituents on a national level.

PARTICIPATION IN NATIONAL POLITICS

Bob Menendez's foray into national politics was a pivotal moment in his career, as it enabled him to intensify his support for his constituents and tackle more extensive national concerns. In 1992, he started his journey from state to federal politics when he was elected to the US House of Representatives.Congress of the United States:States: Menendez ran for and was elected to the 13th District of Congress from New Jersey in 1992. After taking over for Frank Guarini, he made a name for himself in Congress as a proactive and powerful member. While serving in the House, Menendez continued to vigorously support immigrant rights and concentrated on a variety of topics, such as healthcare, education, and economic growth.

Mary A.clapp

In addition to his ability to work across party lines, Menendez was well-known for his commitment to serving the needs of his diverse district, which includes a large number of immigrant populations. He was an outspoken advocate for comprehensive immigration reform, pushing for laws that would safeguard undocumented children, give avenues to citizenship, and guarantee equitable treatment for all immigrants. immigrants. Roles of leadership leadership Menendez's capacity for leadership was not overlooked. In 2003, he was chosen for the third-highest position in the House Democratic leadership—Chairman of the Democratic Caucus. In this capacity, he contributed to the development of the Democratic Party's legislative programme and strategy in the House, enhancing his power and influencing more aspects of national policy.

 Senate of the United States,States, Menendez replaced Jon Corzine, the newly elected governor of New Jersey, when he was appointed to the U.S. Senate in January 2006 due to his commitment and performance in the House. In order to finish out Corzine's term, Menendez won a special election later that year. He was then re-elected in 2012 and 2018. Menendez persisted in

Mary A.clapp

emphasizing foreign policy, healthcare, and immigration reform while serving in the Senate.

He rose to prominence as a member of the Senate Foreign Relations Committee and eventually became its chairman. He was able to influence U.S. foreign policy through his work on the committee, especially with regard to Latin America and international human rights concerns. concerns. Important Lawsuit Initiatives Menendez's dedication to comprehensive immigration reform has been evident in his legislative endeavours in the Senate. In order to safeguard undocumented immigrants, offer routes to citizenship, and guarantee the humane treatment of immigrant families, he has co-sponsored and supported a number of laws. Notably, he has been a fervent supporter of the DREAM Act, which aims to offer undocumented immigrants who entered the country as minors legal status.

Menendez has been a staunch supporter of immigrant rights throughout his career in national politics. He has used his positions in the House and Senate to advance significant reforms and address issues that immigrant communities around the nation confront. His steadfast

Mary A.clapp

dedication to justice, equality, and the American Dream
is still evident in his work.

Mary A.clapp

CHAPTER 2: IMMIGRATION POLICY BEGINNINGS

Bob Menendez's personal history as the son of Cuban immigrants and his strong relationships with immigrant communities motivated him to dedicate himself early in his political career to immigration issues. His initial endeavours in this field laid the foundation for his subsequent, increasingly notable position as a nationwide proponent of all-encompassing immigration reform.

First Position on Immigration Menendez has been an outspoken advocate for immigrant rights since the beginning of his political career. As a Union City, New

Mary A.clapp

Jersey, local politician, he was well aware of the difficulties experienced by immigrant families, especially those from Latin America. His early efforts were centred on making sure these areas had access to possibilities for economic progress as well as basic amenities.

Initial Lawmaking Initiatives Menendez supported immigration-improving legislation in the New Jersey General Assembly and the State Senate. He recognised that these were vital areas where state policy could have a major impact and supported initiatives to give immigrant families better access to housing, healthcare, and education. Menendez maintained his focus on immigration issues after being elected to the US House of Representatives in 1993. He made addressing the concerns of undocumented immigrants and their families one of his first legislative priorities.

His policies have always been to safeguard immigrant workers from exploitation, give legal avenues for undocumented immigrants, and facilitate the reunification of families who have been divided by immigration restrictions. Promotion of All-Around Immigration Reform As Menendez grew in experience and stature in Congress, his dedication to comprehensive immigration reform became increasingly apparent. He backed multiple important bills that changed the immigration laws in the United States.

These initiatives included promoting the legalisation of undocumented immigrants, humanely strengthening border security, and developing an equitable and effective legal immigration system. Menendez was involved in numerous important immigration reform attempts in the late 1990s and early 2000s. He was a strong proponent of the DREAM Act, which was first proposed in 2001 and aimed to offer undocumented immigrants who were brought to the country as minors legal status. Menendez maintained that these people needed to have the chance to completely participate in society because they had no other home and frequently identified as Americans.

Cooperation with Advocacy Organisations To further his legislative objectives, Menendez has collaborated closely with a number of immigrant advocacy organizations over the course of over the course of the course of his the course of his career. His cooperation with these groups has facilitated the representation of immigrant communities' concerns in the legislative process and raised the voices of immigrant communities. Menendez's success as an immigrant reform advocate has been largely attributed to his capacity to develop alliances and collaborate with a variety of groups.

Persistent Attention to Immigration Rights The groundwork for Menendez's ongoing leadership on immigration policy in the US Senate was laid by his early efforts in this area. He is a well-known character in the current national discussion on immigration reform because of his profound comprehension of the difficulties experienced by immigrants and his unrelenting dedication to their rights. Menendez is still an unwavering advocate for immigrant communities and their contributions to American society as he works to implement significant reforms to the immigration laws in the United States.

Mary A.clapp

ORIGINAL IMMIGRATION STANCE

Bob Menendez's early views on immigration were influenced by his close relationships with immigrant communities and his own experiences. Being the son of immigrants from Cuba, he had personal experience with the struggles and hopes of those coming to the US in search of a better life. His early political stances and advocacy work were shaped by this background, which made immigration a major aspect of his career from the start.

Local Politics Advocacy Menendez recognised the needs of his community's sizable immigrant population as soon as he entered municipal politics in Union City, New Jersey. Menendez concentrated on laws that would enhance the lives of immigrants while serving as mayor of Union City and as a member of the board of education for that city. He backed programmes designed to give immigrant families better access to healthcare, housing, and educational opportunities.

Initiatives of State Legislatures Menendez remained an immigrant rights advocate in the New Jersey General Assembly and then the State Senate. He pushed for laws that would facilitate immigrants' assimilation into American society by guaranteeing them access to necessities and chances for career growth.

Among his legislative initiatives were: Education Access: Realizing that education is essential to the success of children of immigrants, Menendez advocated for laws that would give these kids better educational resources and assistance.

Healthcare Services:He backed programmes that addressed the inequities that frequently impacted these areas and increased immigrant access to healthcare.

Housing and job: Menendez worked to advance economic inclusion, fight discrimination, and provide equitable housing and job opportunities for immigrants.

House of Representatives, United States After winning a seat in the U.S. House of Representatives in 1993, Menendez elevated his support for immigrant rights to national prominence. He soon gained recognition for

Mary A.clapp

taking a proactive approach to immigration-related issues, supporting:

Routes of Legalisation:Menendez was a fervent supporter of giving undocumented immigrants legal access. He thought that in order to effectively integrate undocumented people into society and the economy, it was imperative to give them a means of obtaining legal status.

Reunification of Families: He promoted laws that would make it simpler for immigrant families to remain together and help one another, emphasizing the value of family reunion.

Protections for Workers: Menendez backed laws that guaranteed fair labor standards and shielded foreign workers from exploitation. He worked to protect their rights because he understood the important contributions that labor from immigrants made to the economy.

Public Advocacy and Legislative Action Menendez's dedication to comprehensive immigration reform was evident in his early legislative endeavors in Congress. In an effort to improve the fairness and humanity of the American immigration system, he backed a number of measures and initiatives. His public campaigning frequently emphasized the need to treat immigrants with respect and dignity on both a moral and financial level.

DREAM Act:Menendez was an early proponent of the DREAM Act, which aimed to offer undocumented immigrants who entered the country as minors legal status. He maintained that these youths, who frequently saw America as their home, needed to have the opportunity to completely participate in society.

All-encompassing Immigration Reform:Menendez has continuously advocated for comprehensive immigration reform that would have protected immigrants' rights, provided avenues to citizenship for those without documentation, and balanced border security measures.

Cooperation with advocacy organizations organizations Menendez worked closely with immigrant communities and advocacy organizations when he first took an immigration stance. He collaborated with these groups to learn about their issues and take their viewpoints into account while formulating his policy stances.

By working together, he was able to garner widespread support for his proposals and guarantee that his legislative efforts were based on the actual experiences of immigrants. A strong dedication to justice, fairness, and opportunity for all immigrants defined Bob Menendez's early immigration policy. His early campaigning served as a springboard for his later, more comprehensive attempts to safeguard the rights of immigrant communities across the country and modify the immigration laws in the United States.

EARLY POSITIONS AND EFFORT IN THE LAW

As the son of Cuban immigrants, Bob Menendez's dedication to addressing the rights and concerns of immigrant populations informed his early legislative efforts. He also drew on his skills in municipal politics. During his early years in state and federal legislatures,

Mary A.clapp

he supported a number of programmes meant to better the lives of immigrants and advance social justice.

State Legislature of New Jersey Menendez addressed several issues impacting immigrant populations while serving in the New Jersey State Senate and General Assembly. Among his legislative initiatives were:

Access to Education: Menendez promoted laws that would increase immigrant families' children's educational options and guarantee that they had access to high-quality instruction and social assistance.

 Equity in Healthcare: In order to address inequities and obstacles to healthcare services that impacted immigrant groups, he backed policies that would increase access to healthcare for immigrants.

Rights of Employment: Menendez advocated for fair labor practices and laws that forbade workplace exploitation while working on legislation to defend the rights of immigrant workers. His work in the state assembly showed his dedication to supporting laws that supported inclusivity and opportunities for immigrants in

Mary A.clapp

New Jersey, and it prepared the way for his subsequent efforts on the national front.

The United States House of Representatives After winning a seat in the U.S. House of Representatives in 1993, Menendez carried on his support of immigration rights and broadened the scope of his legislative programme to include more national concerns. Among his initial congressional legislative endeavors were the following:

Reform of Immigration: Menendez was an early proponent of comprehensive immigration reform, pushing for laws that safeguarded immigrant families, gave legal status to undocumented immigrants, and catered to the needs of immigrant workers.

Reunification of Families: Realizing the value of keeping families together and promoting their absorption into American society, he backed policies that facilitated family reunification. Initiatives for Social Justice:: Menendez supported laws that attempted to advance equality and social justice, such as initiatives to stop discrimination and guarantee civil rights protections for all people, irrespective of immigration status. During his time in the House, Menendez was able to forge bipartisan coalitions and work with advocacy organizations to further his legislative goals. His early stances on social justice and immigration served as a springboard for his eventual leadership in the US Senate on these topics.

Important Themes Menendez's stances throughout his early legislative career were distinguished by his dedication to:

Inclusivity: Making certain immigrant populations have access to chances for social and economic mobility as well as necessities services.

Equity: reducing inequalities and supporting laws that advance justice and fairness for all people, regardless of immigration status.

Action: Being a strong supporter of social justice and comprehensive immigration reform, he uses his position as a state and federal legislators to bring about significant change. Bob Menendez was committed to advancing policies that enhanced equality and opportunity for all Americans, as seen by his early

Mary A.clapp

legislative efforts and positions. He also represented the concerns of immigrant populations. His leadership in social justice and immigration reform in the US Senate is being shaped by his support for these causes.

CHAPTER 3: MAJOR LEGISLATIVE EFFORTS

Bob Menendez has participated in major legislative initiatives focused on social justice, foreign policy, healthcare, and immigration reform across his career. Millions of Americans' lives have been influenced,influenced, and national policy has been shaped by his leadership in these areas. Here are a few of his most significant bills:

REFORM OF IMMIGRATION

1. ""Comprehensive Immigration Reform"": Throughout his time in Congress, Menendez has been a steadfast

Mary A.clapp

supporter of comprehensive immigration reform.The
legislation he has supported has improved border
security measures, given undocumented immigrants a
path to citizenship, and reformed visa policies to better
serve families and companies.

2. The DREAM Act: Menendez has been a prominent
proponent of the DREAM Act, which seeks to offer
undocumented immigrants who were brought to the US
as minors legal status. He has fought to guarantee
these people's rights and give them chances to make a
positive impact on society.

3. Family Reunification: Menendez has pushed for laws
that give priority to reunifying families, which enables
immigrant families to remain together and assist one
another in the US.

MEDICAL CARE

1. The Affordable Care Act (ACA):Menendez was
instrumental in the enactment and execution of
Obamacare, the Affordable Care Act. He backed
initiatives to increase healthcare coverage accessibility

Mary A.clapp

and shield individuals with pre-existing medical issues
from discrimination.

2. Healthcare Equity: Menendez has fought to eliminate
inequalities in healthcare and guarantee that all
Americans, especially communities of immigrants, have
access to high-quality medical care.

INTERNATIONAL RELATIONS

1. Senate Foreign Relations Committee: Menendez has
shaped US foreign policy as a member and chairman of
this committee, with an emphasis on Latin America and
international human rights concerns.

2. Promotion of Democracy and Human Rights: In
keeping with his commitment to international justice and
security, Menendez has pushed for laws that support
democracy, human rights, and stability in nations all over
the world.

Justice for All

Mary A.clapp

1. Civil Rights and Equality: Menendez has been a steadfast supporter of legislation aimed at ensuring that all Americans have equal protection under the law and fighting discrimination.

2. Criminal Justice overhaul: Menendez has pushed for laws that would improve equity, lower recidivism, and address sentencing inequities in an effort to overhaul the criminal justice system.

FINANCIAL GUIDANCE

1. Consumer Protections: To protect Americans from predatory activities and to guarantee a fair marketplace, Menendez has fought for financial reforms and consumer protections.

2. Job Creation and Economic Growth: Menendez has backed legislation intended to provide opportunities for working families nationwide as well as job creation and economic growth.

Significance and Heritage Significant progress has been made in areas such as foreign relations, healthcare access, social justice, immigration reform,

Mary A.clapp

and economic fairness because of Bob Menendez's legislative initiatives. His leadership continues to influence federal policy on important issues impacting millions of Americans and to shape congressional discussions.

Acts of Comprehensive Immigration Reform Throughout his time in Congress, Bob Menendez has been a leading proponent of comprehensive immigration reform. Although there hasn't been a single comprehensive immigration reform measure solely bearing Menendez's name, he has participated in a number of legislative initiatives and backed comprehensive reform proposals that sought to solve a number of immigration-related issues.

Menendez is linked to the following noteworthy comprehensive immigration reform initiatives:

1. The Immigration Reform Act of 2006 (Comprehensive):This bipartisan initiative sought to strengthen border security, restructure visa policies, and give undocumented immigrants a route to citizenship, but it failed. Menendez backed this legislation and

persisted in pushing for more reforms of a similar nature in the years that followed.

2. The 2013 ""Group of Eight Immigration Reform Bill"": Menendez was one of eight senators from both parties that collaborated to draft a comprehensive immigration reform plan in 2013. The plan includes measures for employment verification, legal immigration system improvements, border security, and a road to citizenship for undocumented immigrants. Despite having bipartisan support, the bill failed to progress in the House of Representatives after passing the Senate.

3. The DREAM Act (Development, Relief, and Education for Alien Minors): The DREAM Act has played a major role in efforts to modify immigration rules while not being a fully comprehensive immigration reform act. Menendez has long been a proponent of the DREAM Act, which aims to give undocumented immigrants who were brought to the US as minors legal status and a route to citizenship.

 4. Various Legislative Efforts: Over his career, Menendez has co-sponsored and supported a number of bills and amendments that address various aspects of

Mary A.clapp

immigration reform, including protections for young people without legal status, family reunification, enhancements to visa programmes, and all-encompassing answers to the problems that immigrants encounter in the United States. Bob Menendez has been a steadfast and outspoken supporter of comprehensive immigration reform, which demonstrates his dedication to establishing a just and equitable immigration system that is consistent with the opportunity and inclusiveness that define American ideals.

Menendez is still advocating for significant legislative answers to the intricate issues surrounding immigration policy in the US, despite the fact that comprehensive immigration reform has proven difficult to achieve at the federal level. DREAM ACT AND DACA Recognising the value of DACA (Deferred Action for Childhood Arrivals) and the DREAM Act in granting chances and protections to undocumented immigrants who arrived in the country as minors, Bob Menendez has been a leading proponent of both programmes.

Mary A.clapp

This is a summary of his work with the DREAM Act and DACA: Deferred Action for Childhood Arrivals, or DACA, Through executive order, President Barack Obama established DACA in 2012, granting work permits and temporary protection from deportation to qualifying undocumented immigrants who entered the country as minors. These individuals are commonly referred to as "Dreamers."

 Bob Menendez has been an outspoken advocate for DACA, fighting to keep the programme intact in the face of legal challenges and attempts to abolish it. His support consists of: Menendez is a co-sponsor of legislation in Congress that seeks to codify DACA into law, giving Dreamers long-term protections and a route to citizenship. He has contributed to the push for comprehensive immigration reform that takes Dreamers into account.

Public Declarations and Advocacy: Menendez has made public remarks in favor of DACA recipients, emphasizing their value to the United States and the necessity of preventing their deportation. He has underlined how morally necessary it is to give young immigrants who

Mary A.clapp

were raised in the US stability and opportunity. Legal
Challenges: Menendez has taken part in legal actions to
protect DACA in court, arguing in favor of the
programmeprogramme's continuance and opposing
attempts to terminate it.

Development, Relief, and Education for Alien Minors Act
(DREAM Act) The DREAM Act is a piece of legislation
that has been brought up repeatedly in Congress with
the intention of giving undocumented immigrants who
were brought to the country as minors road to legal
status and eventually citizenship. Menendez has been a
steadfast advocate for the DREAM Act and has been
instrumental in securing its passage.

Co-Sponsorship: In the House of Representatives and
the Senate, Menendez is a co-sponsor of the DREAM
Act. In order to gain support for the law and create
momentum for its adoption, he has collaborated with
coalitions from both parties.

Advocacy and Outreach: Menendez has undertaken
outreach initiatives to increase support among
legislators, stakeholders, and the general public, as well
as to increase awareness of the significance of the

Mary A.clapp

DREAM Act. He has underlined the necessity of giving Dreamers who have grown up in the country and made contributions to their communities a route to citizenship.

 Legislative Efforts: Menendez has attempted to obtain safeguards for Dreamers in a number of legislative negotiations and has advocated for the inclusion of the DREAM Act in comprehensive immigration reform measures.

Bob Menendez's dedication to safeguarding young immigrants and giving them chances to engage fully in American culture is demonstrated by his support for the DREAM Act and DACA. He keeps pushing for legislative measures that would solve Dreamers' situation and guarantee that their contributions are acknowledged in the US. Develop family reunion policies. In the framework of US immigration law, Bob Menendez has been actively involved in promoting measures that facilitate family reunification.

Family reunification, often known as family-based immigration, is a cornerstone of immigration law that permits holders of green cards and other lawful permanent residents to sponsor certain members of

Mary A.clapp

their families for immigration to the United States,Menendez's work on family reunion programmes can be summed up as follows.

LAWSUIT POSITIONS AND EFFORTS

1. Support for Family-Based Immigration Categories: By maintaining and extending family-based immigration categories, Menendez has backed laws and policies that put a priority on family unity. Through these categories, spouses, kids, parents, and siblings may be sponsored for immigration to the US by US citizens and lawful permanent residents.

2. Action Against Family Separation Policies: Menendez has voiced opposition to measures that cause families to be split up, such as the Trump administration's "zero tolerance" policy, which caused immigrant families to be split up at the border between the United States and Mexico. He has argued in favor of compassionate

Mary A.clapp

immigration laws that put the needs of families first and avoid needless division.

3. Promoting All-inclusive Immigration Reform: Menendez has stressed the significance of changing family-based immigration laws to lower visa backlogs, expedite the process for family members to rejoin, and remove obstacles that keep families apart as part of his larger support for comprehensive immigration reform.

4. Legislative Support: Menendez has co-sponsored bills that aim to expedite the processing of family visas, resolve visa backlogs, and guarantee that immigrant families are treated fairly in the immigration system. These bills are intended to safeguard and increase family-based immigration.

5. Public Statements and Advocacy: Menendez has made use of his position to advocate for immigration policies that prioritize family reunion. He has emphasized personal accounts and pushed for laws that acknowledge the vital role that intact families play in the welfare of immigrant communities and their assimilation into American society.

Mary A.clapp

Significance and Heritage Bob Menendez's support of family reunion laws is indicative of his dedication to preserving humanitarian principles and defending the rights of immigrant families. His legislative initiatives seek to improve social cohesiveness, fortify family bonds, and guarantee that fairness and compassion are at the center of American immigration policy. Menendez is committed to promoting laws that support family unity and deal with the difficulties faced by immigrant families navigating the American immigration system while he serves in the Senate.

CHAPTER 4: ADVOCACY AND PUBLIC STANCE

For the entirety of his public service career, Bob Menendez has consistently advocated for and taken a public position on immigration and related problems. His opinions and advocacy demonstrate his strong belief in social justice, equity, and compassion for communities of immigrants. Below is a summary of his public positions and lobbying on important issues:

Mary A.clapp

PROMOTING IMMIGRATION REFORM ADVOCATES

1. ""Comprehensive Immigration Reform"": Menendez has been a strong proponent of comprehensive immigration reform, which calls for improvements to border security, changes to visa policies, and a path to citizenship for undocumented immigrants. He has made an effort to increase support from both parties for legislative measures that deal with the intricacies of the US immigration system.

2. DACA and DREAM Act: Menendez has been an outspoken proponent of the DREAM Act, which provides undocumented immigrants who entered the country as minors with protections as well as a road to citizenship. He has fought to uphold DACA in court and has co-sponsored legislation that would give Dreamers long-term protections.

Mary A.clapp

 3. Family Reunification: Menendez has highlighted the significance of family reunification in immigration policy, supporting measures that permit lawful permanent residents and citizens of the United States to sponsor certain members of their family members for immigration to the country. He has spoken in favor of compassionate immigration laws that put the needs of families first and has opposed laws that split up families.

SOCIAL JUSTICE AND HUMANITARIAN CONCERNS

1. Opposition to Family Separation: Menendez has been adamantly against measures that force immigrant families to be apart, including the "zero tolerance" policy of the Trump administration. He has denounced these actions and pushed for laws that uphold the dignity and rights of people.

2. Advocacy for Refugees and Asylum Seekers: Menendez has consistently backed laws that shield those escaping violence and persecution. He has criticized attempts to limit access to asylum safeguards and spoken in favor of just and effective asylum procedures.

Mary A.clapp

LEADERSHIP IN LAW AND POLICY INITIATIVES

1. Legislative Sponsorship and Co-Sponsorship: Menendez has been a sponsor and co-sponsor of laws that seek to advance social justice, safeguard immigrant rights, and modernize the American immigration system. His legislative efforts have mostly addressed the backlog of visa applications, expedited the processing of visas, and guaranteed equitable treatment of immigrants within the immigration system.

2. Public Statements and Media Engagement: In order to promote his views on immigration and related topics, Menendez regularly appears in public and speaks with the media. He makes use of his position to advocate for legislation, give firsthand accounts of immigrants who have been negatively impacted by laws, and spread awareness of immigrant rights.

Significance and Heritage The public positions and activism of Bob Menendez on immigration and social justice have greatly influenced national policy discussions and legislative outcomes. He is still an outspoken supporter of humanitarian ideals, immigrant

Mary A.clapp

rights, and legal measures that preserve justice and equality for everyone.

His leadership in the U.S. Senate is indicative of his dedication to advocating for immigrant communities' concerns and advancing laws that uphold the principles of justice, opportunity, and diversity that are inherent to American culture. Public Addresses and Declarations Regarding Immigration Throughout his career, Bob Menendez has made numerous public speeches and declarations on immigration, which is indicative of his fervent support for immigrant rights and comprehensive immigration reform.

Themes and illustrations from his talks and declarations in public on immigration include the following:

1. Deferred Action for Childhood Arrivals (DACA): Menendez has passionately spoken in favor of DACA recipients, or "Dreamers," emphasizing their contributions to American society and advocating for the enshrinement of safeguards in legislation.

Mary A.clapp

 - He has opposed legal challenges that put the DACA program meme's survival in jeopardy and has denounced attempts to revoke the ram.

2. Advocacy for Comprehensive Immigration Reform: Menendez has continuously urged comprehensive immigration reform, which should include improved border security measures, changes to visa policies, and a pathway to citizenship for illegal immigrants.

- In order to solve the intricacies of the American immigration system and establish a decent and equitable path for immigrants, he emphasizes in his lectures the necessity of bipartisan cooperation.

3. Opposition to Family Separation Policies: Menendez has denounced measures that force immigrant families to live apart, including the Trump administration's "zero tolerance" border policy. He has made speeches criticizing these practices as cruel and contrary to American ideals, and he has pushed for laws that put the preservation of intact families first.

4. Support for Refugees and Asylum Seekers: Menendez has expressed his agreement with laws that

Mary A.clapp

shield those escaping violence and persecution in their native nations. In order to guarantee the equitable and effective processing of asylum claims and the availability of humanitarian protections, he has urged for improvements to the asylum system.

5. Promotion of Diversity and Inclusion: Menendez frequently highlights in his remarks the value of diversity and inclusion in American culture, emphasizing the contributions that immigrants have made to the country's social, cultural, and economic fabric. He supports laws that extend a warm welcome to newcomers and recognise the variety that makes American communities stronger.

6. Legislative Advocacy and Appeal to Action: Menendez urges Congress to prioritize legislative solutions that address the needs of immigrant communities and preserve American ideals of justice and fairness. He makes this appeal in his speeches.

- He promotes public support for measures that give immigrants stability and chances to succeed, as well as bipartisan cooperation. Public remarks and speeches made by Bob Menendez on immigration highlight his leadership and dedication to promoting laws that safeguard immigrant rights, support humanitarian principles, and encourage thorough reform of the United States immigration system. His support for immigration reform continues to influence national discussions and legislative initiatives.

WORKING WITH GROUPS THAT ADVOCATE FOR IMMIGRATION

Throughout his career, Bob Menendez has worked closely with a number of immigration advocacy organizations to promote legislative proposals, uphold immigrant rights, and elevate the voices of immigrant populations. His stance on immigration issues has been greatly influenced by his relationships with these organizations.

Here are a few instances of his work with organizations that support immigration:

Mary A.clapp

1. Coalition Building and Legislative Advocacy:
Menendez has collaborated extensively with both
national and local organizations that support immigrants,
including America's Voice, the National Immigration Law
Centre (NILC), and the American Immigration Lawyers
Association (AILA). Together, we have worked to create
and advance laws that address family separation policy,
safeguard DACA recipients and Dreamers, and support
comprehensive immigration reform.

2. Policy Development and Expertise: Menendez has
conferred with immigration advocacy organizations in
order to gain a deeper comprehension of the obstacles
encountered by immigrant populations and to integrate
their viewpoints into proposed legislation.

- Through these collaborations, he has been able to
ensure that legislation pertaining to immigration policy
takes into account the practical effects on immigrant
families and communities.

3. Public understanding initiatives and media
engagement: In order to increase public understanding
of immigration-related issues and rally support for
legislative action, Menendez has taken part in public

awareness initiatives run by immigration advocacy organizations. He has participated in media interviews with advocacy organizations to talk about the significance of upholding immigrant rights and passing comprehensive immigration reform.

4. Legal Support and Defence: Menendez has backed advocacy organizations' initiatives to offer legal support and defense to immigrants who are either facing deportation or applying for asylum. He has opposed acts and policies that endanger immigrant communities and has worked with advocacy organizations to use the legal system to hold these practices accountable.

5. Community Engagement and Outreach: To hear the issues raised by immigrant populations and give updates on legislative initiatives, Menendez has taken part in town halls, community forums, and other events hosted by immigration advocacy organizations.

These interactions have allowed Menendez to speak directly with individuals who have been impacted by immigration laws, which has informed his legislative objectives and strategies. All things considered, Bob Menendez's cooperation with immigration advocacy

Mary A.clapp

organizations shows his dedication to working with interested parties to achieve laws that safeguard immigrant rights, advance social justice, and reform the immigration laws in the United States. His leadership on immigration matters in the U.S. Senate has been boosted by these collaborations, which have also bolstered his lobbying efforts.

PART IN SENATE HEARINGS AND COMMITTEES

Bob Menendez is a major player in a number of important Senate committees, influencing foreign policy, banking, and housing legislation. Thanks to his positions, he can speak out on important challenges that the US and the world community are facing.

Below is a summary of his accomplishments and involvement in Senate committees:

Mary A.clapp

1. Ranking Member: Menendez plays a crucial role in determining American foreign policy as the ranking member of the Senate Foreign Relations Committee. In the areas of international relations, world diplomacy, and US foreign aid initiatives, he is in charge of hearings and legislation.

2. Advocacy for Human Rights: Menendez pushes for laws that advance freedom and equality globally, as well as human rights and democracy abroad. He takes advantage of his position to assist vulnerable groups, including migrants and asylum seekers, and to handle humanitarian disasters.

3. Oversight and Accountability: Menendez supervises the State Department and the carrying out of American foreign policy. In order to hold administrations responsible for their decisions and acts that have an impact on foreign affairs, he holds hearings.

SENATE COMMITTEE ON BANKING, HOUSING, AND URBAN AFFAIRS

Mary A.clapp

1. Senior Member: Menendez concentrates on economic policy, banking regulations, and housing issues that impact Americans across the country in his capacity as a senior member of the Senate Banking, Housing, and Urban Affairs Committee.

2. Consumer Protections: To protect people and families from predatory loan practices and unstable finances, he is a champion for consumer protections and financial reforms.

3. Housing Policy: Menendez focuses on urban growth, homelessness, and affordable housing with the goal of enhancing housing options and circumstances for all Americans.

ADDITIONAL COMMITTEE PARTICIPATION

1. Senate Finance Committee: Menendez serves on the Senate Finance Committee, where he has an impact on laws pertaining to Social Security, trade, taxes, and finance for healthcare.

 2. Urban Affairs, Housing, and Banking Committee: He focuses on housing, banking regulations, and economic policy issues in this capacity.

3. Natural Resources and Energy Committee: In this instance, I have addressed

Mary A.clapp

CHAPTER 5: CHALLENGES AND CONTROVERSIES

Throughout his political career, Bob Menendez has encountered a number of difficulties and scandals that have drawn notice and investigation.

The following are some noteworthy issues and disputes surrounding him:

1. Legal Concerns and Ethics Inquiries: Menendez was accused of accepting gifts and campaign contributions from a wealthy contributor in exchange for political favors, which led to federal corruption charges against him in 2015. He was charged with abusing his position to influence policy decisions in a way that favored the

contributor. The Justice Department dismissed all charges in 2018 after the case ultimately resulted in a mistrial in 2017.

2. Disciplinary Actions and Senate Ethics Committee: Menendez's activities concerning his association with the donor in question were examined by the Senate Ethics Committee. The Senate Ethics Committee "severely admonished" him for his actions, but it did not take any further action even though the case ended without a conviction.

3. Disputes over Policies and Partisan Issues: Menendez has been embroiled in political and policy battles, especially in relation to his support for comprehensive immigration reform and his views on global affairs. These differences have occasionally sparked contentious discussions and condemnation from rival political parties.

4. Challenges in Politics and Campaign Finance Matters: Menendez, like a lot of politicians, has been under investigation for his involvement in campaign financing matters, such as special interest group contributions and fundraising methods. These problems

Mary A.clapp

have periodically called into question his integrity and compliance with campaign funding laws.

5. Public Views and Media Attention: Menendez's political career has been portrayed differently in the public and media as a result of the controversy surrounding him, especially the allegations of corruption and the conclusions of the Senate Ethics Committee. He has successfully negotiated these occurrences both legally and politically, which has been a tremendous task. Bob Menendez has been representing New Jersey as a U.S. Senator since 2006, in spite of these difficulties.

He has stayed true to his beliefs on important issues and is still a powerful force in Congress, representing his people's interests and taking part in committee work on legislation. Legal roadblocks and political opposition Throughout his Senate tenure, Bob Menendez has confronted tremendous political opposition and legislative impediments. These difficulties have frequently revolved around divisive topics, including foreign policy, immigration reform, and ethical disputes.

Mary A.clapp

The following are some salient features of the legislative impediments and political resistance he has faced:

OPPOSITION TO POLITICS

1. "Partisan Divides": Menendez has often faced resistance from other political figures, especially on matters where partisanship is strong. For instance, Republicans and conservative organizations that support harsher immigration laws have vehemently opposed his support for comprehensive immigration reform, which would include providing undocumented immigrants with a road to citizenship.

2. Ethics Controversies: Menendez's political position has been severely harmed, and his opponents have gained ammunition as a result of the federal corruption accusations and the Senate Ethics Committee's ensuing inquiry. Even though there was no conviction in the case, political rivals have continued to criticize the ethical concerns.

Mary A.clapp

3. Campaign Opposition: Menendez has encountered well-funded opposition from Republican contenders and political action committees (PACs) in his reelection campaigns. These groups have attempted to take advantage of the controversy surrounding Menendez and question his leadership and policies.

OBSTACLES IN THE LAW

1. "Gridlock and Partisan Deadlock": Menendez has faced legislative obstacles in Congress, where ideological disagreements and partisanship have frequently prevented advancement on important legislative initiatives. A bipartisan compromise has proven elusive as political differences have impeded efforts to enact major legislation such as comprehensive immigration reform and healthcare reform.

2. Interest Group Resistance: Interest organizations and lobbyists representing businesses or constituencies opposed to Menendez's proposed reforms have resisted his legislative agenda. These organizations have actively opposed his policies and pushed legislators to veto or amend laws that would have an impact on their interests.

Mary A.clapp

3. Complex Policy Debates: It can be difficult for legislators with opposing points of view to find common ground in complicated policy debates, including topics like foreign policy, healthcare, and economics. Entrenched positions and competing interests have hampered Menendez's efforts to advance policy solutions in several areas.

Resilience and Leadership Bob Menendez has persevered and shown leadership in advancing his policy goals and defending the rights of his New Jersey people in spite of these obstacles. With his membership on important Senate committees, such as the Senate Banking, Housing, and Urban Affairs Committee and the Senate Foreign Relations Committee, he continues to actively influence national policy.

Menendez's resolve to pursue his legislative agenda and tackle pressing national challenges is demonstrated by his ability to overcome political opposition and legislative obstacles.

Mary A.clapp

DISPUTES AND CRITICISMS ABOUT IMMIGRATION POLICIES

Opponents of Bob Menendez's support for comprehensive immigration reform and rights for unauthorized immigrants have been the source of criticism and controversy regarding his immigration policy.

The following are a few of the disputes and critiques of his immigration policies:

1. Support for Pathways to Citizenship: Menendez has been an outspoken supporter of giving undocumented immigrants a route to citizenship, particularly through comprehensive immigration reform legislation. Opponents contend that these plans favor illegal immigration and give immigrants' interests precedence over those of natives of the United States.

2. Support for DACA and DREAM Act: Menendez has been controversial in his support of the DREAM Act and DACA (Deferred Action for Childhood Arrivals). Critics

contend that by providing benefits to those who entered the nation illegally and encouraging illegal immigration, these programmes may displace opportunities for lawful permanent residents of the United States.

3. Border Security: Menendez has backed stronger border security measures as part of broader immigration reform, even as he has pushed for citizenship options. His plans, according to his detractors, fall short of what is necessary to protect American borders and stop illegal immigration.

4.Menendez has voiced opposition to stringent enforcement methods that specifically target undocumented immigrants. These policies include mass deportations and the strong implementation of immigration laws without taking humanitarian issues into account. His position, according to his detractors, encourages illegal immigration and undercuts law enforcement.

5. Ethics Controversies: Although not directly connected to immigration policy, Menendez's ethics scandals—such as the accusations of federal corruption and the conclusions of the Senate Ethics

Mary A.clapp

Committee—have stoked criticism of his advocacy and leadership in the field of immigration. These controversies have been used by his detractors to cast doubt on his reliability and judgement.

6. Public Perception and Media Coverage: Menendez's ethical and political controversies have shaped public opinion and media coverage of his immigration policies. Occasionally, unfavorable media coverage has eclipsed his policy stances and lobbying endeavors in this domain.

Bob Menendez is still an advocate for laws that he thinks will simplify the immigration laws in the United States and give undocumented immigrants a chance to assimilate into the country's society, in spite of these objections and disputes. He continues to seek bipartisan solutions to the country's immigration problems and is a strong advocate for comprehensive immigration reform and protections for immigrant communities.

Mary A.clapp

CHAPTER 6: KEY ACHIEVEMENTS AND IMPACTS

Throughout his career, Bob Menendez has made a number of significant contributions and achievements, mostly in the fields of immigration reform, healthcare, and international affairs.

Here are a few of his noteworthy accomplishments and effects:

DIPLOMACY AND INTERNATIONAL RELATIONS

1. Chairmanship and Leadership: As a member and past chairman of the Senate Foreign Relations

Mary A.clapp

Committee, Menendez has greatly influenced American foreign policy and diplomacy. His leadership has had an impact on laws and discussions surrounding topics like global security, human rights, and international aid.

2. Advocacy for Human Rights: Menendez has been a strong global voice in favor of laws that advance democracy, individual freedom, and safeguards for disadvantaged groups. He has pushed for accountability and brought attention to violations of human rights using his position.

3. Support for Global Health Projects: Menendez has backed financing and legislation for global health projects, such as the fight against infectious diseases like malaria and HIV/AIDS. His lobbying has helped the United States take the lead in humanitarian aid and global health programmes.

SOCIAL POLICY AND HEALTHCARE

1. The Affordable Care Act (ACA): Menendez contributed to the enactment of Obamacare, sometimes referred to as the Affordable Care Act, which extended healthcare coverage to millions of Americans and

instituted improvements to the affordability and quality of healthcare.

2. Medicare and Medicaid Advocacy: Menendez has been a steadfast supporter of preserving and growing Medicare and Medicaid, two programmes that offer health insurance to millions of elderly, underprivileged, and disabled persons.

ADVOCACY AND REFORM FOR IMMIGRATION

1.Comprehensive Immigration Reform Efforts: Menendez has been a strong proponent of comprehensive immigration reform, which includes changes to visa policies and a pathway to citizenship for undocumented immigrants. He has made an effort to increase support from both parties for legislative measures that will solve the problems with the American immigration system.

2. Support for DACA and DREAM Act: Menendez has advocated for protections and pathways to citizenship for undocumented immigrants who entered the country as children (Dreamers) and has been a prominent supporter of both the DREAM Act and DACA (Deferred

Mary A.clapp

Action for Childhood Arrivals). His activism has assisted in drawing attention to the Dreamers' predicament and in the campaign for legislative measures that would grant them legal status.

CONSUMER PROTECTION AND ECONOMIC POLICY

1. Consumer Financial Protection Bureau (CFPB): Menendez has backed the establishment and growth of the Consumer Financial Protection Bureau, an organization that ensures fairness in financial transactions and shields consumers from deceptive financial practices.

2. Banking and Housing Policies: Menendez has worked on legislation to support affordable housing, bolster banking rules, and shield customers from fraudulent lending practices while serving as a member

Mary A.clapp

of the Senate Banking, Housing, and Urban Affairs Committee.

THE EFFECT ON NEW JERSEY

1. Transportation and Infrastructure: Menendez has succeeded in obtaining federal funds for transportation-related projects in New Jersey, including upgrades to highways, bridges, and transportation networks, all of which have helped the state's transportation infrastructure and economy.

2. Environmental Protection: Menendez has backed financing and legislation for conservation and environmental protection programmes in New Jersey, including cleanup operations for contaminated areas and the preservation of natural habitats.

The accomplishments and effects of Bob Menendez attest to his dedication to promoting laws that advance economic opportunity, social fairness, and international stability. He still has a big say in determining national policy and attending to the interests of his New Jersey people as a senior senator and committee member.

Mary A.clapp

SUCCESSFUL CHANGES IN POLICIES AND LAWS

During his time in the U.S. Senate, Bob Menendez has been involved in a number of legislative initiatives and policy reforms that have proven effective.

Here are a few noteworthy instances:

1. All-encompassing Immigration Reform Initiatives: Menendez has been a prominent proponent of all-encompassing immigration reform. Menendez has co-sponsored and supported a number of initiatives that try to alleviate the backlog of visas, strengthen border security, and give illegal immigrants a road to citizenship, even if comprehensive reform has not yet passed.

2. Deferred Action for Childhood Arrivals (DACA) defense: Menendez has been a steadfast supporter of DACA participants, fighting for rights and opportunities

Mary A.clapp

for Dreamers—undocumented immigrants who entered the country as minors—to become citizens. Among his initiatives has been co-sponsoring legislation to shield DACA recipients from legal troubles and deportation.

3. International Human Rights and Foreign Relations: Menendez has backed laws and resolutions that seek to further democracy and human rights globally. He has been outspoken about topics like violations of human rights in nations like Venezuela and Myanmar, advocating for international pressure and sanctions to address these transgressions.

4. Advocacy for Medicare and Healthcare: Menendez has argued in favor of maintaining and growing Medicaid, Medicare, and other health care initiatives. He has backed laws that would increase patient protections under the Affordable Care Act, decrease prescription medication costs, and increase access to healthcare services.

5. Reform of Financial Institutions and Rights of Consumers: Menendez has participated in initiatives to improve consumer safeguards and control the banking sector. In order to shield customers from unscrupulous

Mary A.clapp

behavior and avert another financial disaster, he backed
the Dodd-Frank Wall Street Reform and Consumer
Protection Act.

 6. Environmental Protection and Facilities: Menendez
has succeeded in securing federal financing for
transportation system upgrades, bridge construction,
and environmental conservation initiatives in New
Jersey. The state's environmental protections and
infrastructure have improved as a result of his
campaigning.

7. Military Benefits and Veterans' Affairs: Menendez has
backed laws that will give veterans better access to
healthcare, education, and jobs. He has pushed for
more financing for veteran services and benefits, as well
as changes to the VA healthcare system.

8. Crime and Justice Reform: Menendez has backed
initiatives in this area to remove structural injustices in
the legal system, promote rehabilitation programmes,
and lessen mass incarceration. He has co-sponsored
legislation to enhance reintegration programmes for
people who have served time in prison and to change
sentencing rules.

Mary A.clapp

Bob Menendez's commitment to tackling a wide range of issues affecting Americans and advocating for reforms that advance social justice, economic opportunity, and human rights both domestically and globally is demonstrated by these legislative achievements and policy improvements. His efforts have improved the lives of his New Jersey constituents and continue to influence national policy discussions.

WHAT HAPPENS TO IMMIGRANT COMMUNITIES

Bob Menendez's leadership on immigration issues, activism, and legislative achievements have had a tremendous influence on immigrant communities.

He has assisted immigrant communities and affected policy in the following significant ways:

1. Promoting All-encompassing Immigration Reform: Menendez has been a vocal supporter of

Mary A.clapp

comprehensive immigration reform, which calls for improvements to border security, changes to visa policies, and avenues for undocumented immigrants to obtain citizenship. His campaign seeks to give immigrants a just and lawful means to assimilate into American society.

2. Dreamers and DACA Support: Menendez has been an outspoken advocate for Dreamers, or recipients of DACA (Deferred Action for Childhood Arrivals). As an advocate for the contributions DACA applicants have made to American communities and the economy, he has co-sponsored legislation that would shield them from deportation and give them a path to citizenship.

3. Resistance to Family Division Laws: Menendez has been adamantly against measures like the Trump administration's "zero tolerance" policy that cause immigrant families to be split up at the border between the United States and Mexico. He has pushed for laws that give priority to preserving family units and guaranteeing that immigrants are treated humanely.

4. Asylum Seeker and Refugee Advocacy: Menendez has backed laws protecting people who are escaping

violence and persecution in their native countries and are seeking asylum. He has criticized attempts to limit access to asylum safeguards and spoken in favor of just and effective asylum procedures.

5. Legislative Initiatives and Protections: Menendez has co-sponsored legislation that aims to give immigrant communities legal rights and protections. Some of the measures include addressing visa backlogs, shielding immigrant workers from exploitation, and enhancing the availability of legal representation for immigrants who are in danger of deportation.

6. Community Engagement and Support: Through outreach programmes, town hall meetings, and community forums, Menendez actively interacts with immigrant communities. He hears their worries, informs them of legislative initiatives, and offers assistance and tools to help immigrants deal with social and legal obstacles.

7. Legal Aid and Support: Menendez has backed initiatives aimed at giving immigrants who are in danger of deportation or who are applying for legal status access to legal aid and services. He has collaborated

Mary A.clapp

with advocacy organizations to guarantee that immigrants can obtain support services and legal counsel.

Bob Menendez's dedication to supporting laws that preserve immigrant rights, encourage inclusivity, and acknowledge the contributions of immigrants to American society is evident in his influence on immigrant communities. His advocacy on immigration matters continues to influence national discussions and legislative initiatives meant to improve the treatment of immigrant families and communities through overhauling the United States immigration system.

Influence of Border Regions on Domestic Immigration Laws Bob Menendez's leadership positions, advocacy work, and legislative proposals have had a major impact on the country's immigration laws.

He has influenced national immigration policy in a number of ways, including the following:

1. Promoting All-encompassing Immigration Reform: Menendez has been a strong proponent of comprehensive immigration reform, which includes a

number of elements like improved border security, changes to visa policies, and a pathway to citizenship for undocumented immigrants. His lobbying has had a significant role in influencing legislative ideas and encouraging cross-party discussion about immigration reform.

2. Legislative Projects and Collaborative Sponsorship: In order to address the shortcomings of the American immigration system, Menendez has co-sponsored a number of important pieces of immigration legislation. This comprises legislation aimed at safeguarding DACA recipients, giving undocumented immigrants legal status, streamlining the visa application process, strengthening border security, and guaranteeing humane treatment of migrants.

3. Senate Committee Leadership: Menendez has been instrumental in forming immigration policies that touch on foreign policy, economic policy, and national security as a senior member and former chairman of the Senate Foreign Relations Committee, as well as a member of other powerful committees like Banking, Housing, and Urban Affairs.

Mary A.clapp

4. Justification for DACA and Dreamers: Menendez has advocated for legislative protections and avenues to citizenship for Dreamers—individuals who entered the country as children—and has been a prominent supporter of DACA (Deferred Action for Childhood Arrivals) participants. Through his efforts, DACA recipients are now more well-known, and discussions about their contributions to American society and legal status have been influenced.

 5. Resistance to Strict Immigration Laws: Menendez has continuously opposed stringent immigration laws, including those that split up families at the border and limit access to asylum. He has advocated for maintaining humanitarian standards in immigration enforcement and spoken out against attempts to reduce immigrant rights.

6. Advocacy and Coalition Building Groups: In order to increase support for immigration reform and elevate the voices of immigrant communities, Menendez has worked with advocacy groups, organizations dedicated to protecting the rights of immigrants, and other stakeholders. His collaborations with these

Mary A.clapp

organizations have influenced public opinion on immigration issues and helped organize grassroots support.

7. Policy Debates and Public Engagement: Menendez has actively participated in immigration policy discussions through public speeches, media appearances, and legislative hearings, stressing the moral, social, and economic benefits of changing the immigration system. His advocacy has helped to change the political agenda and the public conversation around immigration policy.

Bob Menendez's commitment to establishing a more just and equitable immigration system that strikes a balance between security and compassion and acknowledges the contributions of immigrants to the United States is demonstrated by his wider influence on national immigration policy. His leadership continues to influence legislative initiatives and provide Congress with the impetus for comprehensive immigration reform.

CHAPTER 7: CASE STUDIES

The role of Bob Menendez and his influence on immigration law and associated matters,First Case Study: Dreamers and DACA Background. Undocumented immigrants who entered the country as minors were granted work permits and temporary protection from deportation with the implementation of Deferred Action for Childhood Arrivals (DACA) in 2012. These people, referred to as Dreamers, were born and raised in the United States and frequently view it as their only home.

MENENDEZ'S POSITION:

Mary A.clapp

1. Legislation and Advocacy: Bob Menendez has co-sponsored legislation that aims to safeguard Dreamers and give them avenues to citizenship. He has also been an outspoken supporter of DACA participants. He has backed legislation such as the DREAM Act, which would provide qualified Dreamers with legal status.

 2. Actions Taken by Law: Menendez has taken an active position in the legislative process to enact comprehensive immigration reform that includes Dreamer provisions. In order to rectify their legal situation and guarantee that they are able to fully participate in American culture, he has tried to develop bipartisan support for legislative remedies.

3. Public Litigation: Menendez has advocated for the rights of Dreamers and brought attention to their predicament by using his platform. He has opposed attempts to remove DACA protections and highlighted the social and economic advantages of integrating Dreamers into American communities and employment.

Mary A.clapp

COMPREHENSIVE IMMIGRATION REFORM CASE STUDY

2 .History: A comprehensive immigration reform programme would address border security, legal immigration routes, undocumented immigrants, and enforcement practices, among other facets of the immigration system in the United States. It aims to increase border security and expedite visa procedures while giving undocumented immigrants a route to citizenship and legal status.

MENENDEZ'S POSITION

1. Committee Leadership: Menendez has taken the lead in crafting comprehensive immigration reform legislation as a member and past chairman of the Senate Foreign Relations Committee as well as other committees. He has introduced and co-sponsored laws that deal with the intricacies of the immigration system by using his positions.

2. Building Coalitions: Menendez has developed bipartisan support for comprehensive immigration reform by collaborating with stakeholders, advocacy organizations, and other senators. To reach an agreement on matters like border security, visa changes, and citizenship pathways, he has engaged in discussions and made concessions.

3. Advocacy for Legislation: Menendez has backed legislative efforts that put an emphasis on family reunification, guard against worker exploitation, and guarantee the rights of those involved in immigration processes to due process. He has pushed for laws that honor America's heritage as an immigrant nation and represent humanitarian principles.

These case studies highlight Bob Menendez's proactive involvement in immigration policy, his support of marginalized immigrant groups, and his pursuit of legislative solutions that strike a balance between security concerns and justice and compassion. His leadership still has an impact on Congress's policy decisions and the national dialogue about immigration reform.

Mary A.clapp

Individual Accounts of Refugees Impacted by Menendez's Work I am an AI language model, so I don't have access to the first-hand accounts of people who have been impacted by the activities of particular MPs.

But based on the evidence at hand, I can offer an overview of how Bob Menendez's policies—like DACA and comprehensive immigration reform—have benefited immigrants:

1. DACA Beneficiaries (Aspirants): Thanks to the safeguards offered by DACA, many individuals who entered the country as minors have been able to seek higher education, obtain legal work, and engage in their communities without worrying about being deported. Thousands of people have benefited from Bob Menendez's support for safeguarding Dreamers and giving them routes to citizenship, enabling them to pursue their goals and find stability in the US.

2. Families Reunited by Reforms in Visa Policies: Menendez has backed changes intended to shorten the backlog of visas and expedite the reunion process for relatives of legal residents and citizens of the United States. Families split up by immigration hurdles have

been reunited thanks to these measures, enabling loved ones to be together and support one another.

3. Safeguarding Vulnerable Immigrant Groups: Vulnerable immigrant groups, such as those seeking protection under international refugee rules, victims of human trafficking, and asylum seekers escaping persecution, have benefited from Menendez's efforts to preserve humanitarian values in immigration policy. His effort has made it possible for these people to be treated fairly and to exercise their rights to due process as guaranteed by US law.

4. Legal Protections and Worker Rights: Menendez has backed laws that seek to ensure equitable compensation, secure working conditions, and safeguard immigrant workers from exploitation. His support for comprehensive immigration reform incorporates clauses that protect immigrant workers' rights and make companies liable for labor infractions.

These instances show how policies backed by Bob Menendez have positively benefited immigrant communities by offering opportunities, protections, and avenues to legal status in the United States, even

Mary A.clapp

though individual personal experiences are not available here. An examination of particular bills and their results The Development, Relief, and Education for Alien Minors Act, or DREAM Act, seeks to give undocumented immigrants who were brought to the country as minors (often referred to as "Dreamers") legal status and a route to citizenship.

In the end, it grants permanent residency to those who satisfy specific requirements, such as finishing high school, proving their moral character, and pursuing further education or military duty.

BOB MENENDEZ'S ROLE

Menendez has co-sponsored the DREAM Act for a long time. As a vital piece of legislation that will safeguard and give possibilities to Dreamers—American citizens who have grown up here but do not yet have legal status—he has actively pushed for its approval.

Mary A.clapp

- Menendez has advocated for the DREAM Act through speeches, news conferences, and parliamentary maneuvers designed to garner support from both parties and negotiate concessions in order to move the bill through Congress.

1.Result:The DREAM Act has had difficulty passing both chambers of Congress despite several tries. Although there have been occasions when versions of the bill have received support from both parties, procedural obstacles and political differences on immigration policy have kept the bill from becoming law.

Menendez's efforts have elevated the subject of Dreamers' legal status and increased public awareness and support for protections for this vulnerable demographic, along with those of other senators and advocacy groups. The DREAM Act continues to be a central topic in discussions on immigration reform, with efforts to develop legislative solutions that strike a balance between humanitarian concerns and border security issues being made.

2. All-encompassing Immigration Adjustment
Background:- Comprehensive immigration reform refers

Mary A.clapp

to legislative initiatives meant to address a number of aspects of the U.S. immigration system, such as improvements to visa processing, border security enhancements, legal immigration channel reforms, and pathways to citizenship for undocumented immigrants.

Bob Menendez's Position: Menendez has spent his entire Senate career as a leading proponent of comprehensive immigration reform. In an effort to offer a comprehensive response to the difficulties and complexities of the immigration system, he has co-sponsored and supported comprehensive reform proposals.

- Menendez has leveraged his role as a member of the Senate Foreign Relations Committee and other powerful committees to initiate and advance comprehensive immigration reform legislation. In an attempt to reach an agreement on immigration policy, he has participated in bipartisan talks and coalition-building activities.

Result:Partisan differences, conflicting agendas, and shifting political environments have all made it difficult to enact comprehensive immigration reform.
Comprehensive legislation that addresses all aspects of

Mary A.clapp

immigration policy has proven elusive, even in spite of bipartisan support for some reform initiatives.

Menendez's lobbying and leadership have shaped the national dialogue on immigration reform and advanced certain provisions—like better visa programmes, safeguards for Dreamers, and humane considerations in enforcement practices. Even though comprehensive reform is still a ways off, Menendez is still a strong advocate for legislative measures and keeps talking with interested parties to find workable solutions for immigration law that uphold American goals and values.

 Bob Menendez has demonstrated his dedication to advancing reform initiatives, defending immigrant rights, and looking for bipartisan solutions to the problems facing the American immigration system through his legislative work on legislation like the DREAM Act and comprehensive immigration reform.

Menendez's leadership has significantly shaped the national conversation and advanced policies that seek to offer opportunities and safeguards for immigrants in the United States, despite difficulties in enacting these laws.

Mary A.clapp

CHAPTER 8: FUTURE LOOK

1.Political Dynamics and the Legislative Environment: Menendez's capacity to push immigration reform and other legislative goals will be greatly influenced by the makeup of Congress and the political climate. The chances of implementing comprehensive immigration reform or specific immigration legislation will be impacted by shifts in party dominance, bipartisan cooperation, and electoral results.

2. Public Opinion and Advocacy Activities: The legislative agenda on immigration will continue to be influenced by public opinion and advocacy activities from business groups, immigrant rights organizations, and other stakeholders. Getting public support and

engaging with these groups will be essential for Menendez to build momentum for legislative improvements.

3. Executive Actions and Administrative Rules: The President and federal agencies will execute executive actions and administrative rules that will influence DACA protections, immigration enforcement, visa processing, and refugee admissions. The outcomes of policy and legislative tactics will be influenced by Menendez's oversight responsibilities in Congress and his reactions to executive actions.

 4. Global Migration Trends and International Relations: International ties, migratory patterns, and world events will all have an impact on US immigration policy. Menendez is in a position to discuss international immigration issues, such as regional cooperation on migration concerns, asylum policies, and refugee resettlement, because of his position on the Senate Foreign Relations Committee.

5. Ethical and Legal Considerations: Menendez's political position and ability to influence policy results may be impacted by ongoing ethical issues and legal

Mary A.clapp

difficulties, especially those relating to his prior scandals. Credibility and leadership on immigration and other issues will depend on continued openness and respect for moral principles.

6. Economic and Social Impacts: Discussions about immigration reform policy will take into account the economic contributions of immigrants, labor shortages, and social integration. In order to shape legislative outcomes that benefit immigrant communities as well as the larger community, Menendez's support for measures that strike a balance between economic interests and humanitarian concerns will be essential.

 Bob Menendez's ability to successfully manage political obstacles, forge bipartisan consensus, rally public support, and effectively push for legislative improvements will determine his future influence on immigration and policy matters. The direction of U.S. immigration policy in the coming years will be determined by his leadership on immigration issues as well as changing dynamics in Congress and popular opinion.

Mary A.clapp

PERMANENT RESEARCH AND INITIATIVES

Bob Menendez is still very much involved in continuing projects and activities concerning immigration and other important policy topics.

Menendez is making a major contribution to the following active projects and efforts:

1. All-encompassing Immigration Reform: Menendez is still dedicated to promoting comprehensive immigration reform that improves humanitarian protections, fortifies border security, addresses the legal status of illegal immigrants, and modifies visa policies. He is still collaborating with advocacy organizations and colleagues on the other side to foster understanding and push for legislation.

2. Defense of Dreamers and DACA Recipients: Menendez is still fighting for legal safeguards and avenues for DACA recipients—also known as Dreamers—who were brought to the country as minors

Mary A.clapp

to obtain citizenship. He is in favor of legislative initiatives such as the DREAM Act, which would grant Dreamers permanent legal status and enable them to fully participate in American culture.

3. Family Reunification and Visa Reforms: Menendez is actively working to clear the backlog of visa applications and expedite the procedure so that families can visit their loved ones in the United States. He is in favor of changes that put the needs of families first and guarantee that immigration petitions are processed fairly and quickly.

4. Humanitarian Issues and the Protection of Refugees: Menendez supports laws that safeguard human rights when enforcing immigration laws, shield refugees from harm, and advance global cooperation in the resettlement of refugees. He keeps an eye on events impacting asylum seekers and refugee admissions and responds accordingly.

5. Consumer Protections and Economic Policy: Menendez focuses on economic policies that affect consumer rights, affordable housing, and access to financial services in his capacity as a member of the

Mary A.clapp

Senate Banking, Housing, and Urban Affairs Committee.
He is in favor of laws that defend consumers against
predatory lenders and bolster their rights.

 6. Medicare and Medicaid Accessibility: Menendez is a
supporter of preserving and enhancing access to
healthcare, and he has spoken up against changes and
cuts to Medicare and Medicaid that might prevent some
groups from receiving adequate coverage. He is in favor
of initiatives to expand access to affordable healthcare
for all Americans and reduce the cost of prescription
drugs.

 7. International Human Rights and Foreign Relations:
Menendez is still active in international relations matters,
supporting causes related to global health, democratic
advancement, and human rights. He advances
American leadership on international issues and
addresses international difficulties in his capacity as a
member of the Senate Foreign Relations Committee.

8. Accountability and Oversight by Law: Menendez
oversees the application of laws and regulations
pertaining to immigration, healthcare, financial
regulation, and other important sectors as part of his

Mary A.clapp

role in legislative oversight and accountability. He strives
to make sure that government activities are accountable
and transparent. Bob Menendez's continuous endeavors
are indicative of his extensive policy preferences,
dedication to legislative modification, and support of
marginalized communities.

In order to make significant progress on important
issues affecting Americans and immigrant communities,
he keeps up his efforts in bipartisan cooperation, public
outreach, and legislative strategy.

FUTURE LEGISLATION PROSPECTS

1. "Comprehensive Immigration Reform": Menendez
may keep pushing for comprehensive immigration
reform, which would protect immigrant rights and foster
family unity by improving border security, reversing visa
policies, and providing undocumented immigrants with a
path to citizenship.

2. DACA and Dream Act Legislation: Given his long-standing support for Dreamers, or DACA recipients, Menendez might advocate for legislation that would give Dreamers—those who were brought to the US as minors—permanent legal status and a route to citizenship.

3. Family Reunification and Visa Backlog Reduction: Menendez may be in favor of laws that prioritize family harmony and expedient immigration processing by cutting down on visa backlogs and simplifying the procedure for families to reunite with loved ones in the United States.

4. Healthcare Access and Affordability: Menendez, who advocates for healthcare access, might back laws that safeguard and increase healthcare access, reduce the cost of prescription drugs, and fortify patient rights under the Affordable Care Act (ACA).

5. Consumer Financial Protection: Menendez might keep pushing for changes to secure consumer data privacy, stop predatory lending practices, and guarantee equitable treatment in financial transactions.

Mary A.clapp

6. Environmental Protection and Infrastructure:
Menendez maybach laws that combat climate change,
encourage the use of renewable energy sources, and
fund infrastructure upgrades that increase
environmental sustainability and generate employment.

7. International Human Rights and Foreign Relations:
Menendez might be in favor of legislation that would
improve international democracy, enhance human
rights, and bolster American diplomacy in the world.
This is because he sits on the Senate Foreign Relations
Committee.

8. Military Benefits and Veterans' Affairs: Menendez
might support policies that expand access to healthcare,
education, and work for veterans, as well as
improvements to the VA's support services and
healthcare system.

Menendez's continued dedication to promoting laws that
advance social fairness, economic opportunity, and
international stability is reflected in these prospective
legislative goals. The public's support, partisan
collaboration, and the changing political climate in

Congress will all be critical factors in determining the outcome of these projects.

LEGACY AND IMPACT ON
IMMIGRATION REFORM OVER TIME

Bob Menendez's tenacious lobbying, legislative endeavors, and leadership on significant issues impacting immigrant communities have molded his legacy and long-term influence on immigration reform.

The following are a few elements that add to his legacy:

1. Promoting All-encompassing Immigration Reform: Throughout his career, Menendez has been a steadfast supporter of comprehensive immigration reform. His support highlights the need for a well-rounded strategy that takes border security concerns into account while giving illegal immigrants a road to citizenship and legal status.

Mary A.clapp

2. Dreamers and DACA Support: Menendez's immigration campaign has been anchored on his support for DACA participants, or Dreamers. He has supported legislative initiatives aimed at preventing Dreamers from being deported and giving them the chance to completely assimilate into American society via employment, education, and naturalisation.

3. Coalitions and Legislative Initiatives: Menendez has backed and co-sponsored a number of immigration-related initiatives that seek to protect immigrant workers, alter visa requirements, and address humanitarian issues with immigration enforcement. For the purpose of advancing legislative solutions, he has frequently worked to forge bipartisan alliances and include stakeholders.

4. Impact on Public Policy Discourse: By emphasizing the economic contributions of immigrants, fighting for the humane treatment of migrants, and supporting laws that preserve America's values as a nation of immigrants, Menendez's leadership on immigration has changed public policy discourse.

5. Legal and Social Protections: Menendez has backed initiatives to strengthen legal safeguards for immigrants, such as those aimed at preserving due process rights in immigration procedures, facilitating better access to legal counsel, and preventing family separations at the border.

 6. Humanitarian and International Considerations: Menendez has discussed worldwide immigration issues as a member of the Senate Foreign Relations Committee, including trends in global migration, asylum laws, and refugee resettlement. His advocacy demonstrates his dedication to humanitarian ideals and his leading position on international human rights matters.

7. Community Engagement and Support: By interacting with immigrant communities via town hall meetings, outreach initiatives, and alliances with advocacy organizations, Menendez has made sure that immigrant voices are heard and that their issues are taken into consideration during legislative discussions.

Bob Menendez's consistent dedication to supporting compassionate and comprehensive policies that support

Mary A.clapp

immigrant rights, foster family unity, and acknowledge the contributions of immigrants to American society is what defines his career in the field of immigration reform. The enduring legislative reforms that are implemented and the favorable adjustments made for immigrant communities throughout the United States will serve as indicators of his long-term influence.

CONCLUSION

Bob Menendez's leadership, lobbying, and legislative actions have significantly advanced immigration rights. The following enumerates his principal contributions:Menendez has been a major proponent of comprehensive immigration reform, endorsing laws that aim to strengthen border security, give illegal immigrants a path to citizenship, and restructure visa policies to accommodate humanitarian and economic requirements.

Menendez has been an outspoken advocate for Dreamers, or recipients of DACA (Deferred Action for Childhood Arrivals). In order to prevent Dreamers from being deported and to give them the chance to engage

Mary A.clapp

in the workforce and pursue education, he has
co-sponsored legislation.Menendez has co-sponsored
and supported legislation that aims to reform the
immigration system. Some of the proposals include
better access to legal representation for immigrants
facing deportation, addressing visa backlogs, and
safeguarding immigrant workers from exploitation.

Menendez has placed a high priority on humanitarian
issues when it comes to immigration policy, supporting
measures that protect the right to due process, stop
family separations at the border, and guarantee that
migrants are treated humanely while they are in
detention and during enforcement actions. Menendez
has sought to foster bipartisan support for legislative
solutions and immigration reform by working across
party lines. His endeavors have encompassed reaching
agreements and interacting with others to discover
shared perspectives on intricate immigration
matters.Through town hall meetings, collaborations with
advocacy organizations, and public outreach, Menendez
actively engages immigrant communities. He pays
attention to their issues, raises their voices during

legislative discussions, and attempts to implement policy proposals that will better serve their needs.

Menendez discusses international immigration issues as a member of the Senate Foreign Relations Committee, including topics such as global migration trends, asylum laws, and refugee resettlement. He supports international collaboration on migration-related issues and U.S. leadership on humanitarian matters. In support of equitable and just policies that preserve immigrant rights, encourage family unity, and acknowledge the achievements of immigrants in the United States, Bob Menendez has made significant contributions to the field of immigration rights. In order to better assist immigrant communities and preserve America's ideals as a nation of immigrants, his leadership continues to influence national discussions and legislative initiatives pertaining to immigration reform.

www.ingramcontent.com/pod-product-compliance
Lightning Source LLC
Chambersburg PA
CBHW050802250726
48653CB00006B/2037